c. 1493. Play by Terence, French

c. 1495. City vista, Italian

1560. Bartolomeo Neroni

c. 1765. Gianfrancesco Costa

c. 1770. Bernardino Galliari

c. 1775. Domenico Fossati

ACKNOWLEDGEMENTS: *Albertina, Vienna: 28 right. Bibliotheque Nationale, Paris: 23 right. Cooper Union Museum: 17 top right, 24, 24 left, 26, 29, 34 right, 38 top. David Hays Collection: 43 right. Metropolitan Museum of Art, photo by Francis G. Mayer: 30, 36. Jo Mielziner Collection: 43 left. Museo Nazionale, Naples: 10. Donald Oenslager Collection, photo by Francis G. Mayer: 16, 41, 42 top right, 43 top and bottom right. The publisher also wishes to thank Mr. Oenslager for permission to use certain drawings from his collection as documentation for the end papers. Praun Photos, Munich: 34 left. Rijksmuseum, Amsterdam: 14. Oliver Smith Collection: 42 left. Richard P. Wunder Collection: 28 left. Illustration on p. 19 after the reconstruction by C. Walter Hodges; on page 20 after a drawing by Inigo Jones in the collection of the Duke of Devonshire.*

ABOUT THE END PAPERS: *Examples in chronological sequence of the development of scenic design from ancient Greece to the present day. These vignettes are based on contemporary prints or drawings and on other original documents. The designer's name is given whenever known.*

THE HISTORY OF THE THEATER

BY HANNELORE MAREK

ILLUSTRATED BY PETER SPIER

THE ODYSSEY PRESS · NEW YORK

theater — *From the Greek θεασθαι,*
it means roughly "a place for seeing." —Encyclopaedia Britannica

Theater satisfies a deep need in man; nothing else will explain its persistence. ■ For more than 2000 years it has been disapproved, attacked, excoriated. At the very moment in history that the Greeks were inventing theater as the Western world knows it, it met with stern criticism. The great statesman Solon insisted that an actor pretending to be someone else was telling lies. And there was no use saying that this was only harmless play. "If we honor that sort of thing in play," said Solon angrily, "some day we will find it happening in our business!" ■ And yet, despite violent attacks,

The finest theater of ancient Greece, at Epidauros, with its round orchestra *(from the Greek "place for the chorus of dancers"), survives from the 4th cent. B.C. It seated 12,000.*

official censorship, epidemics that drove away audiences, and acute financial difficulties, the theater endured. In recent years its death has been predicted with monotonous regularity, but it lives. ■ Curiously, for an institution so often accused of immorality, theater began as religious ritual. It was so with the Hebrews and the Egyptians, and again with the Athenian Greeks. As early as 800 B.C., feasts in honor of Dionysus, god of fertility and wine, were held each year at the foot of sloping vineyards. In such a *theatron* the poet Thespis became the first actor in history when, in 534 B.C., he stepped out of the chorus of men and boys to speak solo lines. It was this newfangled notion of Thespis' that aroused Solon's wrath, never

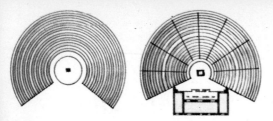

The simple religious rituals of early Greek drama used an unadorned amphitheater with an altar in the center of the orchestra (LEFT). Over some 200 years, plays became more complex and the Hellenistic theater evolved (RIGHT). This had a skene, or stage-building, to serve as a scenic background and to house the actors.

The Greek audience sat on tiers of seats. The chairs in front were for officials.

Greek theater tickets

BELOW, LEFT: A reconstruction of the Greek theater at Eretria. Upper view, from the orchestra, shows the stage building of the Hellenistic period. Lower drawing, a cutaway view from the side, shows the stage building and the stage, the orchestra, and the auditorium.

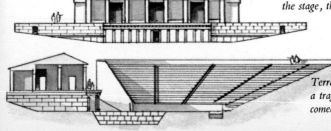

Terra-cotta figures of a tragic hero and 2 comedy drunkards.

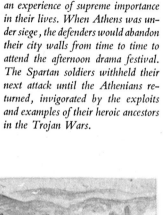

The Greeks regarded theatergoing as an experience of supreme importance in their lives. When Athens was under siege, the defenders would abandon their city walls from time to time to attend the afternoon drama festival. The Spartan soldiers withheld their next attack until the Athenians returned, invigorated by the exploits and examples of their heroic ancestors in the Trojan Wars.

Terra-cotta figure of an actor costumed as a soldier.

before had anyone pretended to be a character in the story the chorus recited. ■ To Solon's disgust, Thespis was a smash hit, and soon Greek theater took on a new form and style; it came to occupy open amphitheaters with stone seats, such as the one below the Acropolis in Athens. There 15,000 people could watch the chorus moving in procession around a circular orchestra and the masked actors on the proscenium platform. Before the eyes of the spectators the great figures of myth and legend came to life: Prometheus, King Oedipus, and the doomed heroes of the Trojan war. Often a *deus ex machina* (literally, a god out of a machine) would descend in a basket operated by pulleys to resolve the tangled complexities of the plot. ■ The six-day dramatic festivals, which citizens attended as a civic duty, incorporated a playwrights' contest. The winner

A reconstruction of the theater at Epidauros.

Roman comic masks: servant, youth, old man.

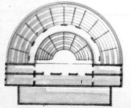

Plan of Roman theater.

Theater ticket of bone.

carried off a generous sum of money and an ivy wreath of victory. The play might be a tragedy in majestic verse by Aeschylus, Sophocles, or Euripides, a light-hearted satyr-play, a comedy-farce by Aristophanes or Menander, or a pantomime of brisk, ribald sketches. ■ After 240 B.C., the theater took new root in Rome and in the cities of its empire. The chorus was eliminated, the altar removed, and the orchestra reduced to a half-circle. The proscenium, or stage proper, jutted out well in front of the scene-building in what would today be called a "thrust" stage. Awnings were stretched across the auditorium to protect the audiences from the direct heat of the morning sun, for all performances took place before noon. ■ The plays were anything but religious in spirit. By the time the first permanent stone theater was constructed in Rome by Pompey, in 55 B.C., popular taste had veered away from the drama toward *spectacula* with their troops of camels and elephants in combat, and naval battles between

Roman theaters were usually built on level ground and were often enclosed. The orchestra was reduced to a semi-circle and the stage enlarged, with an elaborate facade. RIGHT: Reconstruction of Roman theater in Ostia.

real ships on artificial lakes. After 476 A.D. and the ascendance of Christianity, the Church closed all playhouses which it considered bawdy and disreputable. ■ The theaters stood dark, but the theater lived on. Traveling mimes, acrobats and jugglers went up and down the Italian peninsula, crossed the Alps into Provence and the Pyrenees into Spain, and gathered spectators in market places and baronial halls. ■ The same Church that had closed the theaters subsequently revived theatrical art by presenting stories from the life of Christ in song and pageant. From the tenth century on, religion was again the driving theatrical motive. The playlets occupied choir stands, naves, and transcepts, as part of each service. But the congregations, bulked out by visitors, grew too large for the churches, and the productions had to be transferred outside, first to the church steps, porch, and yard, and, by the late 1200's, to the public square. ■ In medieval western Europe —and especially in England—these "miracle plays" based on

The medieval mystery play began as a religious celebration. Later it became a holiday pageant and drew hundreds of visitors from surrounding villages.

Key to the painting of the mystery play opposite identifies nine separate scenes included on a single set. As one episode ended, the actors simply walked across to the next scene, though not necessarily in the following order: (1) Paradise; (2) Nazareth; (3) The Temple; (4) Jerusalem; (5) The Palace; (6) The Bishop's House; (7) The Golden Gate; (8) The Sea; (9) Purgatory and Hell. Performances spread all over a market square, or, as here, the front steps of a cathedral.

13

the lives of Christian saints, "mystery plays" taken from Biblical sources, and "morality plays," in which vices and virtues such as Envy, Pride, and Gluttony were personified, passed slowly from the hands of the clergy to the patronage of the craft guilds. The reason was that this new theater could serve secular as well as pious purposes by attracting travelers and boosting local business. ■ At Coventry, York, and Chester, the guilds put on cycles of 25 to 50 plays which might continue for several days, several times a year. Goldsmiths, water carriers, tailors, and other guild members mounted elaborate productions with expensive apparatus and richly embroidered costumes. The actors, all amateurs, received fees on an accepted scale, the largest sums going to those who took the most exalted roles: God, Jesus, and Mary. During the cycle, each scene, on a movable stage, or "pageant," was hauled into view by horses. ■ Even more ambitious were the "passion plays" put on by an entire community. The most celebrated of these, at Oberammergau in Germany, is still performed; its text has hardly changed for 300 years. ■ In the courts of 15th-

In the 15th century, Renaissance Italy bristled with sumptuous revivals of classical plays. In the Andria of Terence, the four curtains represented the doors to four separate houses. Behind each curtain was a tiny room with a rear window. Thus, flexibility was achieved with the use of only a single set.

15th-century traveling players, performing on a platform stage.

and 16th-century Italy, meanwhile, stagecraft was accomplishing new marvels. The comedies of Plautus and Terence were rediscovered and, for the first time, presented indoors. In the Renaissance theaters, such as the one in the palace of the Duke of Ferrara, an audience of nobles and scholars saw sets painted in perspective, giving the stage an illusion of unity and also of three-dimensional depth. Court productions enjoyed only a single performance, to celebrate a coronation, a royal wedding, or the arrival of a ruler in a city, but expense was not spared. Leading artists, among them Leonardo da Vinci and Raphael, were engaged to design scenery. In 1490, Leonardo developed the revolving stage, which made feasible even more sumptuous masques and other courtly

In this set designed by Sebastiano Serlio in the 1550's, only the steps and the narrow stage are real; the scene is painted in perspective on a backdrop.

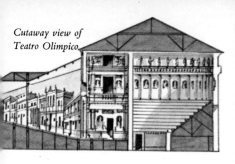

Cutaway view of Teatro Olimpico

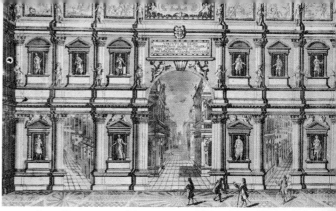

An early engraving of the proscenium of the Teatro Olimpico.

The Teatro Olimpico at Vicenza, Italy, was the most advanced and magnificently equipped playhouse of its time. It had a raked (sloping) stage and five arches, each with its own perspective alley. At least one alley could be seen by each spectator. The auditorium was semi-elliptical rather than semi-circular. The Olimpico was designed by Palladio, who died before it was completed. Scamozzi, who introduced the perspective alleys, completed it in 1584. The design was much admired and was widely imitated all over western Europe. At lower right: the Teatro all' Antica at Sabbioneta, built 1588–90.

Plan of Teatro Olimpico

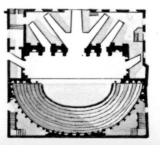

The Bear Garden   *The Globe*

spectacles. The high points, or "intermezzos," might call for gigantic dragons or lions to be lowered from the flies, and the curtain was operated *during* the show to conceal the shifting of properties. In 1521, London welcomed the Emperor Charles V with an indoor sky glittering with stars and angels suspended on clouds. On another occasion, a Florentine audience witnessed colored lighting and fountains and breathed in perfumed smoke. ■ Step by step, the flat backdrop evolved into an open gate through which sliding canvases appeared on rollers, and *periacti,* or three-sided prisms, spun about to reveal different scenes on each face. The Teatro Olimpico at Vicenza, begun in 1580 by the architect Palladio and completed by his son, had a facade of archways, cornices, columns, houses, and temples. But the most mod-

ABOVE: *The Thames River in Shakespeare's day.* LEFT: *Early woodcut of a scene from* The Taming of the Shrew.

The Globe playhouse, most celebrated of all the "public" Elizabethan theaters, stood near the Thames, and equally near its rival, the Hope or Bear Garden. Erected in 1599, it belonged to the company headed by actor-manager Richard Burbage. Today we think of it as Shakespeare's house, since his greatest plays were first presented there. Yet so were the plays of his contemporaries. This cutaway view shows the Globe's polygonal shape, a wooden "O" that seated some 800 spectators in three roofed galleries. Groundlings stood in the pit in front of the three-quarter stage. Above the proscenium a balcony served for the romantic scenes—as a hilltop, a tower, a fortress wall, or merely the upper story of a house. There was no front curtain and "corpses" had to be hauled off quietly at the act's end.

Inigo Jones, the foremost English designer of the 1600's, studied the Olimpico sets and was profoundly influenced by their formally balanced designs and carved proscenium arches. ABOVE: *A copy of a Jones' sketch for a tragic scene.*

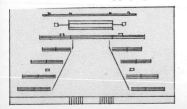

ern theater of the age was the Teatro Farnese at Parma, with its auditorium divided into boxes, galleries, and a pit for standees. ■ In this atmosphere of luxury the play was *not* the thing. It was Spain and England that ushered in new drama, at a time when these two small nations had expanded into the mightiest imperial powers on earth. In Spain, Lope de Vega and Calderôn won over popular and court audiences alike with their cloak-and-sword plots, their vigorous language, and inventive comedy. Lope was a prodigy for any age; he was in turn explorer, sailor, soldier of fortune, roué, and priest. He was credited with over 900 plays, dashed off so swiftly in cadenced verse that, as he said, "more than a hundred passed from the Muses to the theater each in 24 hours." To

Plan and cross-section of the stage for Salmacida Spolia, *designed by Jones. The four sets of side-wings each contained four flats. Behind them were four shutters cutting off the rear stage; behind them, the perspective.*

In the 17th-century theater, a lack of richness in plots was compensated for by lavish and exotic costumes, often inspired by myth, allegory, or the Far East. The designs above are by Ludovico Burnacini, a contemporary of Inigo Jones.

him scenery and machinery only cluttered up a stage; he asked for no more trappings than "four trestles, four boards, two actors, and a passion." ■ Similarly, in England, the Elizabethan playwrights vividly described the time, the locale, and the action in their texts. The imagery of Marlowe, Shakespeare, Jonson, and Webster was so resplendent that any but small properties — flags, swords, etc. — would have seemed an intrusion. Shakespeare's Chorus in *Henry V* entreats the listeners to "piece out our imperfections with your thoughts."

In contrast to the Globe and the Fortune, the private and the court theaters of early 17th-century England, with their wealthy and aristocratic patrons, were famed for their extravaganzas. A masque in the palace of James I in 1618 cost more than 4,000 pounds. Inigo Jones, who had studied the masques and their costumes in Italy, adapted them with many refinements and novelties to the English theater. Jones' three most important innovations were the introduction of lighting (colored glass globes or oiled paper, with candles inside them); the scenic curtains, which, depending on the requirements of each play, might fall at the front, back, or center of the stage, like today's "painted drop"; and the proscenium arch, often prettied-up with sea gods, clouds, nymphs, and "naked children dallying with a drapery," the whole border being inscribed in gold and silver lettering and

In the gardens of the Grand Trianon at Versailles, Louis XIV built an elaborate al fresco theater. At a performance in 1674, he and his family sat front row center, where the sun would shine on them. The drawing here is after an old print. About 100 years later, another theater was built within the palace itself; it was opened with a ball in honor of the marriage of Louis' great-great-grandson, Louis XVI, to Marie Antoinette. RIGHT: *Louis XIV as Apollo.*

23

To change sets quickly, 18th-century designers used devices such as revolving prisms (periacti) *with scenes painted on three sides* (ABOVE), *and flats pulled aside on wheels* (BELOW).

Side and front view of a demon's head, designed by Jean Berain. The jaws opened, and revealed prop flames.

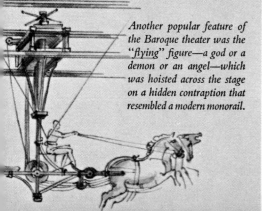

Another popular feature of the Baroque theater was the "flying" figure—a god or a demon or an angel—which was hoisted across the stage on a hidden contraption that resembled a modern monorail.

bold colors. ■ At the Whitehall Theatre in 1660 another Italian importation went on display. This was the *Commedia dell'arte,* a method of improvising comedy which had been flourishing in Italy for about 100 years. In the *Commedia,* performers had a repertory of short sequences, or "scenarios," that could be interchanged at the drop of a cue. It was not a question here of pure ad-libbing, but rather of testing audience reactions and then bringing forth the episodes likely to raise the most and biggest laughs. Each actor specialized in a certain role, which he played in a broad dialect; he wore a particular costume and a recognizable mask of thin leather molded to fit his features. ■ The stock characters of the *Commedia* included Pantalone, an avaricious old

By mid-18th century, scenic design reached a peak of extravagance. The example at far left is by Girolamo Fontana, who designed settings for the elaborate theatricals of the Polish Queen, Maria Casimira, residing in Rome.

25

man from Venice; the pedantic Scholar; Harlequin, the servant, in his diamond-patterned clothes; Columbine, the pretty comedienne; Pierrot, a valet whom life always treated rudely; and an assortment of other figures, from a cowardly but boastful soldier to a pair of incredibly innocent young lovers. ■ The *Commedia* troupes covered a lot of ground, sometimes traveling as far afield as Spain or northern France. One company was offered a permanent theater in Paris, which it later shared with Molière and his players, taking over the house on alternate afternoons. Molière was already acquainted with the *Commedia* routines. He had toured the south of France and seen the Italian comedians playing in Lyon, Marseilles, and other cities. As a result of this knowledge,

A leading character of the Commedia dell'arte *was the mercurial and prankish Harlequin, with mask and wooden sword. He was the perennial lover of Columbine.*

In England a puppet variant on the Commedia sketches was the Punch and Judy show (BELOW). Old hook-nosed Punch traces his descent to Pulcinella, the clown of the Italian theater. Throughout the show Punch belabors his wife with a stick and fights off unexpected assaults by the Devil and other malign visitors. In France, Punch is known as Polichinelle; in Germany, as Kasperle.

The improvised farces known as Commedia dell' arte sprang up in Italy during the 16th century, but many travelers from other parts of western Europe brought back glowing reports, and the Italian players were invited abroad. They then started permanent companies in Paris and London, which persisted until the 18th century. In the masks and clothes that identified them instantly, the Commedia's rich assortment of stock characters included the prankster Coviello (IN TWO VERSIONS, A AND B), Pantalone, the miser from Venice (C), Pulcinella (D), and a pedantic Doctor (E).

Stage and theater design in the 17th and 18th centuries was dominated by *Ferdinando Galli-Bibiena, his seven sons, and grandsons, whose magnificent scenic architecture led to innovations in actual buildings. The sets at left and above have a solid, three-dimensional appearance, but consisted partly of painted flats, cunningly angled and overlapped.*

and also because of his aim "to please the public," many of his 33 plays are studded with Italian gags *(burli)* and bits of business *(lazzi)*.

■ While his great contemporaries, Corneille and Racine, stunned audiences with their resonant but highly disciplined verse tragedies, Molière, who himself produced and directed many of their works, was leading the theater in a second—and a third—direction. The plays he chose to write were comedies that poked fun at misers, hypocrites, braggarts, and fools. But he also had to provide a continual flow of entertainments for Louis XIV, the "Sun King," and his nobles. Thus, some of Molière's plays were given in Paris at the elegantly equipped Petit-Bourbon theater or the Palais-Royal. Others, designed to amuse the courtiers and called comedy-ballets, played at the royal establishments in Versailles and Saint-Germain. With grottoes and palatial sets by Torelli,

The set above is by Filippo Juvara, whose sets are unmatched in originality and boldness. His most important contribution to scenic design was to break away from the tradition of extravagant sets and to introduce more naturalistic scenes. His influence extended beyond the theater to contemporary landscape painters. Juvara, who lived from 1678 to 1736, designed sets for many monarchs of Europe.

This drawing of a stripped-down 18th-century stage reveals its basic construction. On the receding wooden frames, canvas flats would be mounted. The backdrop is already in place. Carpenters are adding beams capable of supporting machines 40 feet wide by 60 feet long. Other carpenters are working on a trap door. The devices for lighting the stage (BELOW) seem to be fairly primitive, but in fact they worked efficiently. The dimmer consisted of two cylinders that were lowered over candles to produce a surprising range of light-intensity; while color effects were achieved with bottles or flagons of tinted water through which candlelight glowed and cast an evenly suffused hue over selected areas of the stage.

music by Lully, fireworks, cannon, gods, centaurs, and other mythical monsters sporting among fountains and in glades, these were productions to overwhelm all the senses at once. The King and the aristocrats liked to participate. They capered about in the ballet interlude of *The Forced Marriage*, for which the King donned the garb of a gypsy; in the *Ballet of Night* he played the sun. After Molière's death, Louis combined his company with its leading competitors to form the Comédie-Française, the world's first national theater. ■ By then baroque was the dominant fashion, made manifest in the almost sensuously curved architecture, the lush gardens, and colonnaded chateaus, and the costumes of Jean Bérain, with their Roman reminiscences, immense skirts, and plumed headdresses. At a period when almost every building was so ornate that it looked like a theater, inside and out, archi-

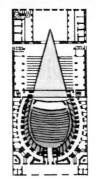 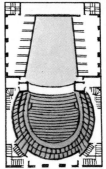 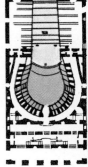

La Scala, Milan   *Théâtre-Français, Paris*   *San Carlo, Naples*

The plans above show three ways in which 18th-century architects sought to enlarge the auditorium without infringing on the space needed for the vast stage and its machines. In attempting to pack in as many spectators as possible, they expanded the traditional semi-circular seating area into a horseshoe shape. As a result, the view of the stage for spectators at the rear and the sides was impaired.

31

To Drottningholm came troupes from France and Italy. So did admiring royal visitors. The theater (ABOVE LEFT) is on the grounds of the summer palace of the Swedish royal family.

Though it is a small house, the Drottningholm Theater has an uncommonly deep stage, which can take seven projecting side wings. The theater was unused for 150 years, but no restoration was needed when it was reopened, beyond replacing the ropes in the machinery. Electric lighting was added, and today it is one of the finest existing examples of the 18th-century theater.

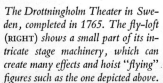

The Drottningholm Theater in Sweden, completed in 1765. The fly-loft (RIGHT) shows a small part of its intricate stage machinery, which can create many effects and hoist "flying" figures such as the one depicted above.

tects moved easily into stage design. One of them, Ferdinando Galli-Bibiena, introduced something most of the great theaters of Europe later adopted: the two wings, or flats, which were painted with such a sharply angled perspective that they gave the impression of an even deeper stage. (Actually, the stage could have used more depth; it accommodated not only the cast and scenery but also favored members of the audience.) As the baroque grew ever more fantasticated and finally passed into the rococo, an era in the French theater came to its end. ■ At the Drury Lane theater in London, David Garrick had been trying for more naturalness in his productions. He trained his actors to avoid histrionics and he simplified

ABOVE: *The auditorium during a recent performance with a set painted by Carlo Bibiena in 1774.* BELOW: *The tent of Agamemnon, in a set made in 1786. Like all the original sets constructed for this theater, it is still in use.*

The Residenz Theater in Munich, designed by Cuvilliés in 1750 for the royal family of Bavaria, was taken apart for safekeeping during World War II and later carefully restored. In the Bavarian baroque style, it has four tiers of loges extending to right and left of the royal box.

Cutaway view of the theater, in a contemporary engraving after a drawing by the architect. Winches and levers controlled the angle of the floor. It could be sloped for theatrical performances, or made flat when the chairs were removed and the auditorium used as a ballroom.

the sets by commissioning "landscape designs," which were so beautifully executed that an artist of the stature of Gainsborough could show himself "wrapt in delight" over them. ■ But the next renewal of the theater came from Germany. During the last 30 years of the 18th century, the "Storm and Stress" movement, sponsored by the Duke of Weimar at his modest court theater, opened the floodgates of 19th century romanticism, which was to inundate the whole of Europe. Goethe, Schiller, Lessing, Kleist, and lesser playwrights took Shakespeare as their spiritual father and wrote about individuals and their personal conflicts, rather than court gossip and mannerisms. These

productions emphasized the text of the play, sometimes at the expense of the acting and theater craftsmanship. ■ Elsewhere in Europe the romantic age witnessed some of the loveliest backcloths ever seen. At the Drottningholm Theatre outside Stockholm, a massive proscenium arch framed exquisite sylvan scenes and delicate, receding streetscapes. In London, Edmund Kean's *Henry VIII* was played in 1854 before a cloth painted by five leading artists of the period; it turned on two rollers to depict the entire length of the Thames. In front of this passing scene sat King Henry in a stationary barge. ■ In France the romantic tragedy arrived like a thunderclap with the plays of Victor Hugo. The first showing, in 1830, of his *Hernani*, whose hero is a bandit, touched off a riot. Angry theatergoers battled with a claque of Hugo's supporters, who were identified by their shaggy beards and pink vests. But

Romanticism soon became the theatrical convention of the day, and its lavish historical trappings were enhanced by gas lighting which, after the 1830's, replaced candles. ■ Up to this time, playwrights had tapped the past for their subject matter or had concocted brittle comedies of manners. Now they attempted a new type of realistic portrayal: contemporary man. Rhetorical dialogue went out. So did artificial sets and stage behavior. Plays looked like an imitation—or, more drastically, a slice—of life. The situations and social problems posed by Ibsen, Chekhov, Shaw, and their followers demanded box sets for the most part, rooms with the fourth wall missing and furnished with utilitarian, everyday props. Scenery was not to

LEFT: *In 1794 London's fashionable Drury Lane Theater was altered, making it the largest of its time. The Prince Regent, his friends, and their mistresses met regularly in the boxes over the stage.* RIGHT: *An opening night in the early 1700's. Unfortunately, the building burned down in 1809.*

Hundreds of published designs by Antonio Basoli, like the one above, spread the neoclassic approach to stage design beyond Italy. A particular feature of early 19th century design was comparatively modest interiors, as required by the increasingly realistic plays of the period.

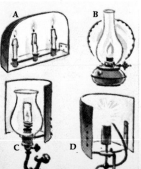

intrude on the action, and definitely not to be admired for its own sake, as it had been during the preceding two centuries. The basement setting of Gorki's *The Lower Depths* conveyed the hard realities of poverty and misery. ■ Realism, or naturalism, fostered by such outstanding directors as Antoine in Paris and Stanislavski in Moscow, has remained the principal form of theatrical expression down to our own day. But it has been complicated and enriched by the infusion of many fresh styles and startling discoveries. Among them are the expressionism of Strindberg and the

Before the discovery of the electric lamp at the end of the 19th century, the theater used four progressively better types of lighting: candles placed in a screen or hood (A); oil lamps (B); gaslight (C); and limelight (D), which was produced by burning lime and which gave a steady, powerful illumination. The court theater in Weimar once used 1100 wax candles for a play by Schiller.

"tragedies of sex" by Wedekind. The dreamlike, almost hallucinatory images and the Freudian overtones of these turn-of-the-century plays profoundly influenced Eugene O'Neill and his contemporaries. ■ The "theater of the absurd" of Beckett, Ionesco, and Adamov in the 1950's has carried drama beyond dreams into nightmares, in which man is the toy of an inscrutable power, a descendant of the Greek hero at the mercy of his pantheon of gods. Thus, over 2,500 years the legitimate theater has come almost full circle. ■ During the past century, the musical, too, has evolved—from the staid, waltzing, Central European operetta into a fullfledged, exciting medium in its own right. Following the lead of *Oklahoma*, with its pacesetting dances by Agnes de Mille, modern musicals incorporate ballet, singers, actors, full orchestra, and fluid staging to produce a total effect. ■ In line with these changes,

Although professional actors from England performed in Williamsburg, Virginia, in 1752, America had few permanent theaters until the 1800's. A unique American institution was the show boat, such as Chapman's Floating Theater, which was launched in 1831.

39

Three-set revolving stage.

Plan of theater with three-set revolving stage and horseshoe-shaped auditorium.

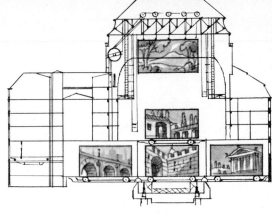

The 20th century has brought a variety of new devices for changing sets quickly. In the Dresden State Theater (ABOVE), opened in 1918, elevator wagon stages are arranged in four separate sections, each of which can be stored above or below the stage proper. In the "combination" set at left, as the play progresses, different parts of the same set are lighted to effect a change of scene.

Robert Edmonds Jones' set for O'Neill's Ah, Wilderness! Jones is one of a remarkable group of American artists, such as Bel Geddes, Oenslager, Simonson, and Mielziner, who brought a new vitality to theater design.

modern settings have abandoned the older, more literal type of representation. Adolphe Appia, Gordon Craig, Norman Bel Geddes and other designers have tried to integrate the direction and the scenery, and have conjured up a timeless, suggestive atmosphere on stage by means of stark, retreating pillars, abstract geometrical shapes and, above all, by the interplay between sets and lighting. ■ Footlights are disappearing, and, thanks to the pioneering of Max Reinhardt in Germany

The English designer Gordon Craig gave the stage a chaste, sculptured look by lighting abstract forms, as in his set for Romeo and Juliet. *He greatly influenced modern design.*

Oliver Smith: Camelot, *1962*

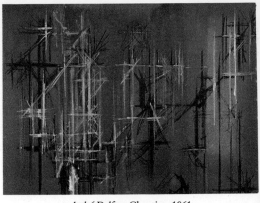

André Delfau: Chantier, *1961*

and Jean Vilar in France, today's stages are illuminated by strategically placed "spots" and "floods." In more advanced theaters, the Loeb at Harvard, for example, an electronic device controls the switchboard with the aid of computer cards. Following preselected cues, this lighting system plays with an infinite variety of effects, from a single spot piercing total blackness, through every conceivable mixing of colors, to brilliant whiteness. ■ Our most modern

Jo Mielziner: The Lark, *1955*

Donald Oenslager: Dido and Aeneas, *1953*

Jean Cocteau once said, "Inspired settings and costumes can make or mar a production." Modern theatrical producers share his opinion, and the designers' sketches on these two pages illustrate some noteworthy achievements of the 20th century. RIGHT: *David Hays' set for O'Neill's Long Day's Journey into Night, 1958.*

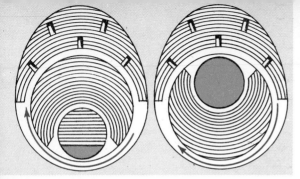

The leader of the European Bauhaus movement in art and architecture, Walter Gropius, applied its "functional" principles to the theater in 1924, and came up with a blueprint for this shell-like auditorium and circular stage (colored blue here). The stage and the banks of seats behind it were to be swung about so that they switched places and formed a theater-in-the-round. Gropius' "total theater" was never built, but has recently been imitated in Finland. One critic noted: "I kept wondering how we must look to the passing birds as we spun around idly in the sunshine."

theaters are thus astonishingly flexible instruments. Their acoustics can be adjusted; their stages have large turntables and can adapt electronically to multiple settings; and the entire auditorium can be rearranged for an arena performance with the spectators surrounding the stage on four sides. More and more of these opulently appointed playhouses are under construction in our cities and universities, some of them as elements in new cultural complexes such as Lincoln Center in New York City. ∎ Despite the competition of television, the movies and opera, the theater triumphantly persists. International festivals, touring companies, and far-seeing exchange programs are carrying its long history and its restless present to new audiences across the world. And the audiences are giving back to the theater its age-old reward: their applause.

INDEX

1776. Vincenzo Mazzi

1786. Josef Platzer

c. 1820. K. F. Schinkel

c. 1912. Adolphe Appia

c. 1924. Aleksandra Exter

1937. Christian Bérard